BREAKOUT BIOGRAPHIES

LEONARDO DICAPRIO

Actor, Environmental Activist, and UN Messenger of Peace

Kristen Rajczak Nelson

PowerKiDS press.

New York

Published in 2018 by The Rosen Publishing Group, Inc.
29 East 21st Street, New York, NY 10010

First Edition

Editor: Elizabeth Krajnik
Book Design: Tanya Dellaccio

Photo Credits: Cover Jon Kopaloff/FilmMagic/Getty Images; p. 5 (top) Jemal Countess/Getty Images Entertainment/Getty Images; p. 5 (bottom) JEWEL SAMAD/AFP/Getty Images; p. 7 Darlene Hammond/Archive Photos/Getty Images; p. 9 (top) Neilson Barnard/WireImage/Getty Images; pp. 9 (bottom), 17 Kevin Winter/Getty Images Entertainment/Getty Images; p. 11 (top) Sunset Boulevard/Corbis Historical/Getty Images; p. 11 (bottom) Ron Galella, Ltd./Ron Galella Collection/Getty Images; p. 13 S. Granitz/WireImage/Getty Images; p. 15 (top) HAL GARB/AFP/Getty Images; p. 15 (bottom) Archive Photos/Moviepix/Getty Images; p. 19 (top) Pool/Getty Images News/Getty Images; p. 19 (bottom) AFP/Getty Images; p. 21 ANNE-CHRISTINE POUJOULAT/AFP/Getty Images; p. 23 (top) Mark Davis/Getty Images Entertainment/Getty Images; p. 23 (bottom) Eduardo Munoz Alvarez/Getty Images Entertainment/Getty Images; p. 25 (top) Jason Merritt/Getty Images Entertainment/Getty Images; p. 25 (bottom) MARTIN BUREAU/AFP/Getty Images; p. 27 Jerod Harris/Getty Images Entertainment/Getty Images; p. 29 Gustavo Caballero/Getty Images Entertainment/Getty Images.

Cataloging-in-Publication Data

Names: Rajczak Nelson, Kristen.
Title: Leonardo DiCaprio: actor, environmental activist, and UN messenger of peace / Kristen Rajczak Nelson.
Description: New York : PowerKids Press, 2018. | Series: Breakout biographies | Includes index.
Identifiers: LCCN ISBN 9781538326237 (pbk.) | ISBN 9781538325537 (library bound) | ISBN 9781508163152 (6 pack)
Subjects: LCSH: DiCaprio, Leonardo–Juvenile literature. | Motion picture actors and actresses–United States–Biography–Juvenile literature.
Classification: LCC PN2287.D4635 R34 2018 | DDC 791.4302'8092 B–dc23

Manufactured in the United States of America

CPSIA Compliance Information: Batch #BW18PK For Further Information contact Rosen Publishing, New York, New York at 1-800-237-9932

CONTENTS

Actor, Activist 4
Leo at Home 6
Starting Out 8
Breakout Star 10
Hitting the Big Time 12
An Eye-Opening Meeting 16
The Foundation 18
Movies with Messages 20
The Oscar 24
Documenting Climate Change 26
Still in the Spotlight 28
Glossary 31
Index 32
Websites 32

ACTOR, ACTIVIST

Leonardo DiCaprio is one of the most famous and respected actors today. He's taken on challenging roles, worked with celebrated directors and actors, and won numerous awards. DiCaprio also speaks out about how people treat Earth and what the consequences of their actions might be.

In 2016, he spoke to members of the United Nations (UN) about the seriousness of **climate change**: "In America I have witnessed **unprecedented** droughts in California and sea level rise flooding the streets of Miami." He said climate change has gotten out of control and the lives of all living things are in danger.

DiCaprio's interest in the **environment** began before he acted in any movies or won any awards. Though he makes his living as an actor, Leonardo DiCaprio is an **activist** at heart.

DiCaprio has traveled all over the world to learn more about how climate change is affecting Earth. Even though he has a busy schedule as an activist, DiCaprio has acted in numerous movies since 1993.

THE PARIS AGREEMENT

On April 22, 2016, DiCaprio spoke to the UN before the signing of the Paris Agreement. In this agreement, countries from around the world promise to fight against and limit human activities—such as burning **fossil fuels**—that are causing climate change to speed up. DiCaprio said, “It will mean nothing if you return to your countries and fail to push beyond the promises of this historic agreement. Now is the time for bold, unprecedented action.”

LEO AT HOME

Leonardo Wilhelm DiCaprio was born November 11, 1974, in Los Angeles, California. He lived with just his mother, Irmelin, for most of his childhood. His father, George, a comic book author, lived nearby. DiCaprio is very close to both his parents. He's said he had a good childhood even though his family didn't have much money.

DiCaprio was on a TV show called *Romper Room* when he was five years old, but it wasn't until he was about 14 years old that he started to seriously think about becoming an actor. He told the *New York Times*: "I knew I didn't want to be one of the set things they said I should be at school—doctor, lawyer, blah blah blah."

In 2015, DiCaprio said that, growing up, he felt close to Hollywood but also far away. He hoped the "higher nobles of the acting world might one day reach out and accept [him]."

STARTING OUT

DiCaprio started his acting career by going to auditions, or tryouts, for commercials. There were many jobs he didn't get. Finally, DiCaprio landed a commercial for Matchbox cars. However, a year went by without him being cast again. Encouraged by his father, DiCaprio passed the time when he wasn't working by watching classic movies. He also made friends with other young actors, such as Tobey Maguire, at auditions.

In 1990, after appearing on a few other TV shows, DiCaprio landed a role on the show *Parenthood*. DiCaprio's first film role was in *Critters 3*, a funny horror movie, which was released in 1991.

Soon after his film career began, DiCaprio was cast as a homeless teenager on the popular TV show *Growing Pains*. The show was canceled in 1992. It would be DiCaprio's last time acting for TV.

TOBEY MAGUIRE

Maguire and DiCaprio have remained friends well into adulthood. The two acted in *The Great Gatsby* together. The movie was shown for the first time at the 66th annual Cannes Film Festival in Cannes, France.

CHOOSING ROLES

DiCaprio now has his choice of acting jobs. In 2011, he spent hours in a makeup chair to look like J. Edgar Hoover, the former head of the Federal Bureau of Investigation (FBI). He told the *New York Times* in 2011 that he likes to take roles other actors might be scared to take: "When I can't immediately **define** the character, and there's an element of mystery to it and still a lot to be explored, that's when I say yes."

BREAKOUT STAR

In 1992, when he was only 17 years old, DiCaprio auditioned for a role opposite the legendary actor Robert De Niro. He said he knew who De Niro was but hadn't studied his movies. DiCaprio walked into the audition room and shouted his lines right in De Niro's face. His strong audition got him the job. *This Boy's Life* came out in 1993 and put DiCaprio in the spotlight.

That same year, DiCaprio played a teenager with mental disabilities opposite Johnny Depp in *What's Eating Gilbert Grape?* The director said DiCaprio's ability to play such a challenging character was evident from his first audition: "[He] was the only one who had picked up on the **essentials**. . . . He was the most observant." DiCaprio received an Academy Award, or Oscar, nomination for best supporting actor for his performance.

DiCaprio was chosen for his role in *This Boy's Life* over many other young actors, including his friend Tobey Maguire.

HITTING THE BIG TIME

Over the next few years, DiCaprio starred in several movies, including *The Basketball Diaries*, a serious independent film based off Jim Carroll's **autobiography** of the same name. *Romeo + Juliet*, released in 1996, was a hit—especially with young women. It made DiCaprio an idol for teens all over the world. In fact, he was chased out of the Louvre, a famous museum in France, by a group of young female fans. Then, along came *Titanic*.

Titanic director James Cameron wasn't even sure he wanted DiCaprio to play the role of Jack Dawson, a lower-class boy who falls in love with an upper-class girl. DiCaprio had to be convinced, too. He wasn't interested in making hit movies. However, after meeting with and charming Cameron and discovering Kate Winslet would be his costar, DiCaprio signed on.

DiCaprio starred opposite Claire Danes in *Romeo + Juliet*. In 1997, he received the Silver Bear award for best actor at the Berlin International Film Festival for his role in the film.

Filming for *Titanic* was long and included 70-hour workweeks. DiCaprio spent a lot of time in a 17-million-gallon (64.4 million L) water tank, which he didn't enjoy. He missed home and his friends, and he was tired of being in Mexico, where filming for *Romeo + Juliet* had also taken place.

When *Titanic* came out in 1997, it was clear the hard work was worth it. The three-hour movie about Jack and Rose falling in love aboard the historic ship became one of the highest-earning movies of all time. It made DiCaprio a genuine star. He was only 23 years old, and his face was on the cover of magazines all over the world.

DiCaprio knew after *Titanic* that hit movies weren't his style. He wanted to be known for more than just his looks.

KATE WINSLET

It was obvious to DiCaprio's friends that *Titanic* was going to be a big deal for his career. Tobey Maguire said at the time: "It's not going to be just 12-year-old girls watching him. It's going to be *everyone*."

WINSLET AND DICAPRIO AS ROSE AND JACK

AN EYE-OPENING MEETING

In 1998, DiCaprio's journey from actor to activist began with a meeting with the vice president, Al Gore. Gore had been speaking out about global climate change since the 1980s. As vice president, he tried to convince Congress and the world how serious the climate situation was. To show DiCaprio how serious climate change is, Gore drew a picture of Earth and its atmosphere on a chalkboard. From that moment, DiCaprio became very interested in the issue. Today, he credits Gore with introducing him to the reality of climate change and putting him on his path to environmental activism.

Not long after this meeting, DiCaprio founded the Leonardo DiCaprio Foundation. The foundation's mission includes "protecting the world's last wild places" and "ensuring the long-term health and well-being of all Earth's inhabitants."

Even before meeting Gore, DiCaprio was interested in helping the environment. He's said that when he was young, he was really sad to learn about animals going extinct, or dying out, because of human actions.

THE FOUNDATION

Since its founding, the Leonardo DiCaprio Foundation has given more than $60 million in grants and worked with more than 65 groups in more than 46 countries around the world. The foundation has supported organizations that work to save animals in danger, such as partnering with the National Park Service on a tracking-collar study of mountain lions in the greater Los Angeles area of California. It works with groups, such as Ocean 5, that want to protect the world's oceans. The foundation also helps indigenous, or native, peoples who want to pursue more equality and to spread their knowledge of the natural world. It also supports people and organizations that are in search of new ways to deal with problems on Earth.

In addition to his own foundation, DiCaprio works with other environmental organizations, including the World Wildlife Fund and the International Fund for Animal Welfare.

DiCaprio met with President Barack Obama on a number of occasions to discuss climate change and the president's environmental policies.

DEADLY SERIOUS

DiCaprio doesn't try to disguise his opinions on climate change. He believes climate change is a real and very scary issue. He told *Rolling Stone*: "I am consumed by this. There [aren't] a couple of hours a day where I'm not thinking about it. It's this slow burn. It's not 'aliens invading our planet next week and we have to get up and fight to defend our country,' but it's this **inevitable** thing, and it's so terrifying."

MOVIES WITH MESSAGES

In 2006, DiCaprio starred in *Blood Diamond*, a movie about a diamond **smuggler** during the Sierra Leone civil war in 1999. He spent six months filming in parts of Africa where he saw a lot of poverty and disease. The experience was eye opening. He said, "You can't help but [be] affected when you're in those locations and seeing that stuff face to face." DiCaprio was nominated for another Oscar for his role in the film.

The following year, *The 11th Hour*, a **documentary** DiCaprio both produced and did voice work in, was released. *The 11th Hour* shows how climate change came to be and how people's lifestyles have affected the earth. DiCaprio interviewed famous scientists, such as Stephen Hawking, and other experts about the issues, including how people can work to save Earth from climate change.

At the Cannes International Film Festival, DiCaprio said of *The 11th Hour*: "We essentially took what the scientists and some of the greatest thinkers in the world had to say and tried to put it into an hour-and-a-half format. . . . My position was to ask the questions and get the real story."

DiCaprio received yet another Oscar nomination in 2013 for his performance in *The Wolf of Wall Street*. He played a dishonest **stockbroker** who took advantage of many people and made lots of money at their expense. Much like many of DiCaprio's other movies, *The Wolf of Wall Street* had a message. He told National Public Radio the movie was about greed in today's world.

By 2014, DiCaprio was well known for his interest in environmental causes. The United Nations named him a messenger of peace, acknowledging his efforts to raise awareness about climate change. When he was given this title, DiCaprio said he felt that he had to speak out about climate change: "How we respond to the climate crisis in the coming years will likely determine the fate of humanity and our planet."

Famous film director Martin Scorsese and DiCaprio worked together on *The Wolf of Wall Street*. Other movies Scorsese and DiCaprio worked on together include *Gangs of New York* (2002), *The Aviator* (2004), *The Departed* (2006), and *Shutter Island* (2010).

WHO ARE MESSENGERS OF PEACE?

The UN names celebrities from many backgrounds, including actors, musicians, authors, and athletes, messengers of peace so they can use their fame to spread certain messages for the UN. DiCaprio is a messenger of peace with a focus on climate change. Celebrated cellist Yo-Yo Ma is a messenger of peace who focuses on bringing music to young people. Author Paul Coelho is a messenger of peace who focuses on poverty and communication between different groups of people.

THE OSCAR

DiCaprio's fifth Oscar nomination for acting came in 2016 for a film called *The Revenant*. He grew a long beard and had to make the audience believe a bear had attacked him. The movie was long, but it earned a lot of praise and won the Golden Globe for best motion picture—drama. The public was strongly rooting for DiCaprio to win the Oscar for best actor. Then, more than 20 years after his first starring role, DiCaprio finally won.

In true DiCaprio fashion, he used his time in the spotlight on the Academy Awards stage to talk about climate change: "Climate change is real, it is happening right now. It is the most **urgent** threat facing our entire species, and we need to work collectively together and stop **procrastinating**."

DiCaprio barely spoke in *The Revenant*. He had to use his face, eyes, movements, and reactions to communicate what he was thinking and feeling as the character.

AWARDS

DiCaprio has been nominated for many awards and won many for his performance in *The Revenant*. Here are just some of the awards he's won over the years:

Golden Globe, best actor:
The Aviator, The Wolf of Wall Street, The Revenant

MTV Movie Awards, best male performance:
Titanic, The Aviator, The Revenant

People's Choice Awards, 2014:
Favorite dramatic movie actor

Screen Actors Guild Awards, 2016, leading actor:
The Revenant

DOCUMENTING CLIMATE CHANGE

While DiCaprio was working on *The Revenant*, he was also hard at work on another climate change documentary called *Before the Flood*. DiCaprio traveled all over the world to see the many locations affected by climate change, including the shrinking polar ice caps and coastal cities being swallowed by flooding. He interviewed experts as well as notable people such as Pope Francis to hear their points of view on the issue.

Having produced two climate change documentaries in addition to his work with his foundation, DiCaprio has been asked why he keeps acting if he's so invested in his causes. He realizes that being a celebrity gives him a bigger platform to spread his message: "One hand shakes the other . . . not that necessarily people will take anything that I say seriously, but it gives you a voice."

DiCaprio released *Before the Flood* before the 2016 presidential election, hoping to make climate change an issue Americans would be concerned about when voting for president.

STILL IN THE SPOTLIGHT

Since the early 1990s, DiCaprio has been in the spotlight. Today, he's known both for his award-winning work as an actor and his tireless efforts as an activist. DiCaprio has no plans to stop working on either. He continues to search for roles that will challenge him as a performer. Through the Leonardo DiCaprio Foundation and the United Nations, he seeks to find even more ways he can reverse climate change's effects on Earth.

In his speech to the UN in 2016, DiCaprio asked world leaders which side of history they'd like to be on. It's clear that DiCaprio is making a name for himself as one who will be on the side of Earth, spreading the message of how to save it for as long as he can, as loudly as he can.

Though movies and environmentalist work take up much of his time, DiCaprio has said he tries to "find balance" and enjoys deep-sea scuba diving and collecting fossils.

TIMELINE

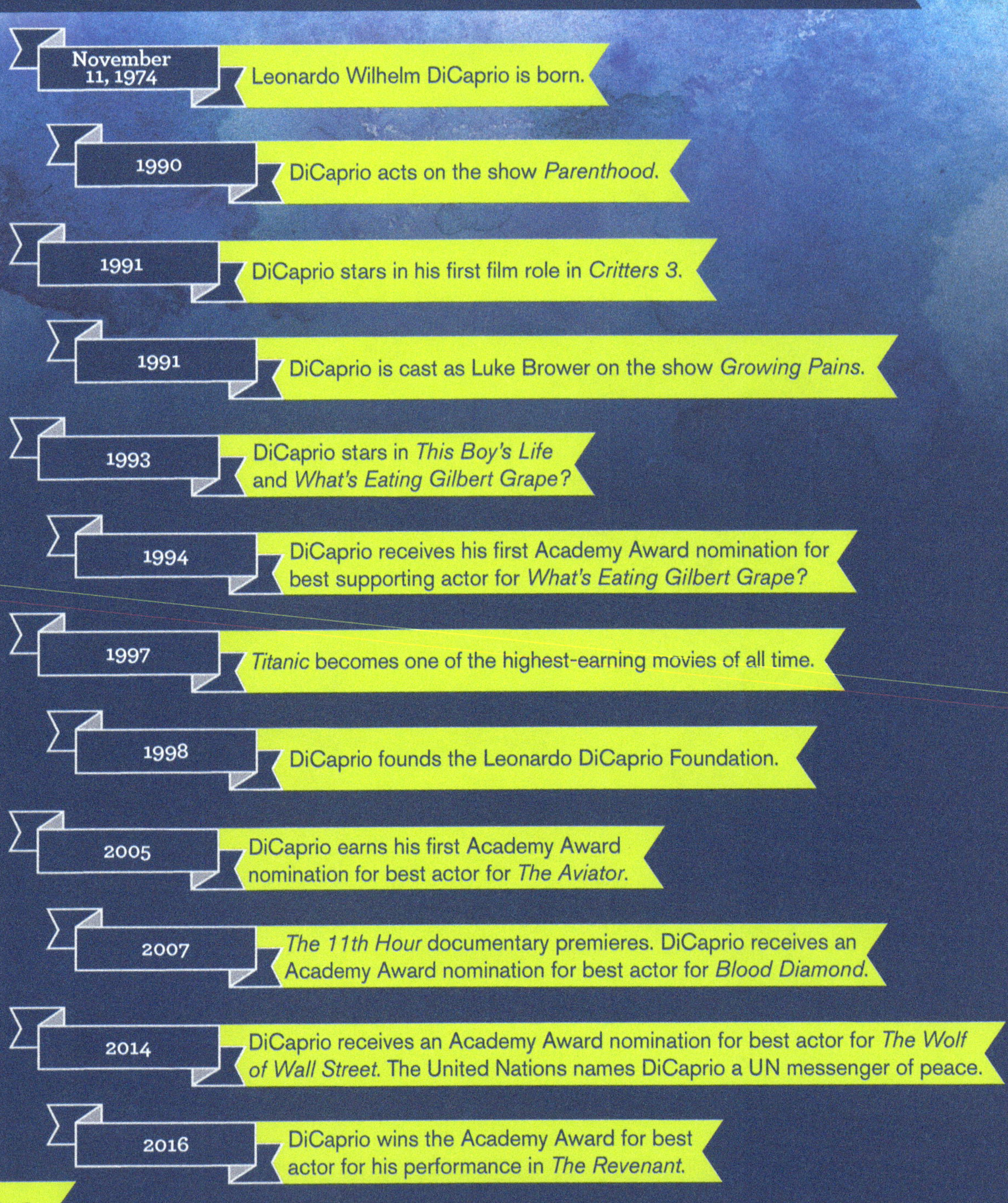

November 11, 1974	Leonardo Wilhelm DiCaprio is born.
1990	DiCaprio acts on the show *Parenthood*.
1991	DiCaprio stars in his first film role in *Critters 3*.
1991	DiCaprio is cast as Luke Brower on the show *Growing Pains*.
1993	DiCaprio stars in *This Boy's Life* and *What's Eating Gilbert Grape?*
1994	DiCaprio receives his first Academy Award nomination for best supporting actor for *What's Eating Gilbert Grape?*
1997	*Titanic* becomes one of the highest-earning movies of all time.
1998	DiCaprio founds the Leonardo DiCaprio Foundation.
2005	DiCaprio earns his first Academy Award nomination for best actor for *The Aviator*.
2007	*The 11th Hour* documentary premieres. DiCaprio receives an Academy Award nomination for best actor for *Blood Diamond*.
2014	DiCaprio receives an Academy Award nomination for best actor for *The Wolf of Wall Street*. The United Nations names DiCaprio a UN messenger of peace.
2016	DiCaprio wins the Academy Award for best actor for his performance in *The Revenant*.

GLOSSARY

activist: Someone who acts strongly in support of or against an issue.

autobiography: A book that tells the story of a person's life and is written by the person it's about.

climate change: Change in Earth's weather caused by human activity.

define: To discover the basic parts or meaning of something.

documentary: A nonfiction movie or television program presenting facts about an issue.

environment: The natural world around us.

essential: Something that is basic or necessary.

fossil fuel: A fuel—such as coal, oil, or natural gas—that is formed in the earth from dead plants or animals.

inevitable: Sure to happen; certain.

procrastinate: To keep putting off something that should be done.

smuggler: A person who moves goods into or out of a country illegally.

stockbroker: A person whose job it is to buy and sell shares of stock for other people.

unprecedented: Not done or experienced before.

urgent: Having or showing a sense of requiring immediate action.

INDEX

A
Academy Award, 10, 24, 30
Aviator, The, 23, 25, 30

B
Basketball Diaries, The, 12
Before the Flood, 26, 27
Berlin International Film Festival, 13
Blood Diamond, 20, 30

C
Cameron, James, 12
Cannes International Film Festival, 9, 21
climate change, 4, 5, 16, 19, 20, 22, 23, 24, 26, 27, 28
Critters 3, 8, 30

D
Danes, Claire, 13
De Niro, Robert, 10, 11
Departed, The, 23
Depp, Johnny, 10, 11

E
11th Hour, The, 20, 21, 30

G
Gangs of New York, 23
Golden Globe, 24, 25
Gore, Al, 16, 17
Great Gatsby, The, 9
Growing Pains, 8, 30

L
Leonardo DiCaprio Foundation, 16, 18, 28, 30

M
Maguire, Tobey, 8, 9, 11, 15
messengers of peace, 22, 23, 30
MTV Movie Awards, 25

O
Oscar, 10, 20, 22, 24

P
Parenthood, 8, 30
People's Choice Awards, 25

R
Revenant, The, 24, 25, 26, 30
Romeo + Juliet, 12, 13, 14
Romper Room, 6

S
Scorsese, Martin, 23
Screen Actors Guild Awards, 25
Shutter Island, 23
Silver Bear award, 13

T
This Boy's Life, 10, 11, 30
Titanic, 12, 14, 15, 25, 30

U
United Nations (UN), 4, 5, 22, 23, 28, 30

W
What's Eating Gilbert Grape?, 10, 30
Winslet, Kate, 12, 15
Wolf of Wall Street, The, 22, 23, 25, 30

WEBSITES

Due to the changing nature of Internet links, PowerKids Press has developed an online list of websites related to the subject of this book. This site is updated regularly. Please use this link to access the list: www.powerkidslinks.com/bbios/dicaprio